C000175976

David Young

A to Z of Villages

From the popular TV series

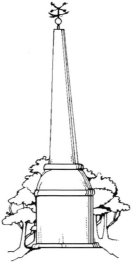

OBELISK PUBLICATIONS

ALSO BY THE AUTHOR:
More… Cobblestones, Cottages and Castles

To Nicholas Bull
a good friend with
a love of the South West
which matches my own

ACKNOWLEDGEMENTS:

I am deeply grateful to Lady Wilson of Rievaulx, who by way of a foreword has allowed me to reproduce, from her collected works, her delightful poem *The West Country*, which sums up not just her love for the South West but also the deep affection all of us share, who are lucky enough to live here.

My thanks also go to:

The Parish councils and Church councils and the people of all the villages featured and in particular to those lovely people who so kindly let me into their homes and establishments;

The National Trust;

Michael Lees for the use of his delightful painting of Clovelly;

TSW who gave me the opportunity of putting the series together in the first place and for the skills of the cameramen and editors who helped make the series;

My wife Margot for the many hours she worked to produced the typescript;

Finally, Sally and Chips Barber, thoughtful, considerate and above all helpful publishers.

PLATE ACKNOWLEDGEMENTS:

Provided or taken by Chips Barber: pages 6, 12, 13, 14 (top), 17, 23, 29, 30, 31, 32, 36, 37, 38, 41, 42, 47, 48, 49, 50, 51, 52, 53, 58, 59 and 61. Michael Lees: page 14 (bottom); Jane Reynolds: page 15; Chris Chapman: page 16; Gillian Williams: page 33; Nicholas Horne: page 34; Eugene Taglione: page 19. All other pictures by or belong to the author.

First published in 1993 by
Obelisk Publications
2 Church Hill, Pinhoe, Exeter, Devon EX4 9ER, England
Design and Layout by Chips and Sally Barber
Typeset by Sally Barber
Reprographics by Equinox
Printed in Great Britain by Maslands Ltd.

© **David Young 1993**
All Rights Reserved

Contents

The West Country

Your winding roads are blocked by cars and trailers,
And trudging feet have worn your headlands bare;
Yet still your deepest lanes are full of flowers
The old West Country magic lingers there.

Your red lands, fold on fold, reach to the sunset,
And singing larks float from the half-grown hay,
And foam creams in across your golden beaches,
And grey slate hamlets head each hidden bay.

Yes, still a land remote, a dream unchanging,
A picture from the past you seem to be;
Far to the West, free from the noise of cities
A long arm stretching out into the sea.

Mary Wilson.

𝔍𝔫𝔱𝔯𝔬𝔡𝔲𝔠𝔱𝔦𝔬𝔫

My *A to Z of Villages* first saw the light of day in Television South West's *'Today'* programme. Such was its success with viewers that the series was reshown several times as 'fillers' between programmes. Since then it has filled similar slots in various television stations throughout the country.

If *your* village is not included, I apologise but would like to point out that, as in every alphabetic list of anything or anywhere, only one of each can be included. I also make no excuse for 'artistic' licence in including Exford as my letter 'X'!

Finally I hope you have as much pleasure in reading the *A to Z of Villages* as I had, both visiting and filming with Labrador companion Oliver, and in writing the series.

𝕬bbotsbury — 𝕯orset

Just behind the Chesil Bank, some sixteen miles of pebble beach stretching from Bridport to Portland, lies the delightful Dorset village of Abbotsbury, famous to summer visitors for its tropical gardens and swannery.

St Catherine's chapel, high on a hill over looking the village, has for centuries served as a beacon and lighthouse, as well as a place of worship.

For over a thousand years now, Abbotsbury, full of houses built of golden coloured stone, has been an important village. It would have reached the status of a town had it not been for the dissolution of the monasteries. The abbey, founded by King Canute's steward, was huge. There was the main church and cloisters surrounded by the ancillary buildings, which included dormitories and the refectory where the monks ate their meals. Sadly the heavy hand of Henry VIII was felt here in Dorset and the abbey buildings were acquired by Sir John Strangways, in whose family's hands it still remains.

So what happened to all the abbey buildings? Where are they? Well, they still surround us in Abbotsbury: they line the streets. People wanting to build their own houses went to the old abbey buildings, pinched the stone, using it as a quarry, and adapted it to build their own homes. They didn't just take the stone; they took doors and windows as well and even items like gargoyles! You really cannot blame them; it was there for the taking. For me that is what makes this such a lovely village – the continuity and colour of the stone.

The abbey ruins were to suffer once more when the abbey house and church were besieged by Cromwell's men during the Civil War. The house was destroyed when the magazine blew up, and little remains apart from the arch to the original gate house.

The church, however, was spared, despite the fact that it was garrisoned by Royalist troops; shots were fired and damage caused. There was a pitched battle inside the church, musket balls flying in all directions; you can still see the chip marks in the pillars, some shot even finishing up in the roof! Holes found as recently as 1930 in the pulpit, were caused by musket balls, and not death watch beetle as had been supposed.

Abbotsbury has always been a caring village; the high pavements were built during the eighteenth century to protect pedestrians from being splashed by passing stage coaches. Mail coaches regularly made their way along the coastal road through the village between Weymouth and Bridport. This was a major coaching route and Abbotsbury an important staging post. Coaches stopped at The Ilchester Arms, a perfect example of a seventeenth century coaching inn.

Don't miss the Abbey barn down the hill from the church, one of the largest in the country. (The barn is covered in detail in my book More...Cobblestones, Cottages and Castles.)

I hope your appetite is sufficiently whetted to visit Abbotsbury for yourself, just one of our beautiful villages in this lovely part of England. Pick a fine day and go and see it for yourself.

Blisland — Cornwall

The way to Blisland on the western fringes of Bodmin Moor is marked by wayside crosses. There are seven in all, and when you consider that there are 360 such crosses in Cornwall, this village certainly has its fair share. The Saxons grouped their houses around the village green, one of very few in Cornwall, so Blisland is Saxon in origin.

Sadly, many of the fine trees were destroyed by Dutch Elm disease. Some did survive and many new saplings have been planted.

The main buildings of the village face onto the green, all of them built of granite. Cottages, several of them Georgian, with their small paned windows, fill the north side of the green together with the village inn. On the west side are the village shop and post office together with the old smithy and stable block. To the east of the green is the ancient mansion house complete with unusual scrolls that look like liquorice allsorts made of granite.

But time hasn't stood still here at Blisland, new houses have been built thoughtfully away from the green, and most with the panelled stonework fit quite well into the village picture.

I have deliberately left the south side of the green until last, for here, alongside the village hall, which was once a school, is the parish church. It is dedicated strangely enough to two brothers martyred in Roman times, St Proteus and St Hyacinth. The church today is known locally as St Pratts. Although it looks like any other Cornish church from

Jesus Christus

the outside, the inside is a revelation. It is ablaze with colour that glows and sparkles, making it look just as it did in medieval times. Colour everywhere, from the stained glass windows to the lovely rood screen that divided the priest from the congregation. This served a practical purpose as well, for it helped to prevent dogs, who were welcome in church at that time, from fouling the altar. It also enabled the priest, in early days before pulpits, to give his sermon from a lofty perch. Lessons were also read before the advent of the lectern.

One of the church's treasures is a fascinating copy of St Veronica's handkerchief. Such items were prized in churches in medieval times. Our Lord stumbled carrying the cross and a lady, Veronica, took compassion on him, wiping his forehead with her handkerchief. Legend is that the face of Our Lord was imprinted upon it. The original handkerchief became a very important relic. It is very popular, because if you look at the face of Our Lord his eyes are closed, if you look hard again they appear to open.

This lovely church is full of such treasures. I have my doubts whether there could be another church interior to compare with it, for when you cross the threshold you step back in time six hundred years.

Clovelly — Devon

These days it is refreshing to find a village unspoilt by overhead lines and other modern utilities that can ruin their appearance. Clovelly's amazing cobbled main street, which tumbles along the line of an old water course to the sea below, has been lucky. Thanks to the presiding Hamblin family, it has been able to maintain its old world character. The sixteenth century cottages were restored and cleverly improved between 1914 and 1925 by Christine Hamblin, and her initials appear on many of the houses.

Transport, strangely enough, was never a problem in this once busy fishing village, for donkeys carried, and still do for that matter, loads up the steep street, whilst sledges are used for the downward journey of goods. They are also used to deliver beer to the New Inn at the top of the village: no easy task, so the beer here costs a penny or two more than anywhere else.

Although Clovelly was recorded in the Domesday Book, George Cary, who died in 1601, is largely responsible for the layout of the village as we see it today; it was built then at a cost of around £2000. He was also responsible for the construction of the harbour, which was reconstructed later in 1795 and lengthened in 1826.

Clovelly offers the only anchorage for many miles, sheltered as it is from the prevailing

Clovelly, Cottages on Beach.

Clovelly, Rose Cottage.

Clovelly, High Street, looking down

NORTH HILL AND BACKSTAIRS, CLOVELLY.

South Westerly gales. Whilst the village remains the same, people change. July and August see an influx of holiday makers who are welcomed to the village, up to seven thousand a day at the height of the season.

A favourite spot for artists, the village has been captured more times by renowned artist Michael Lees than any other painter. Over the years, his much sought-after paintings have captured just about every aspect of the village.

I wondered what the village was like in its heyday as a fishing port? Where better to find out than the bar of the Red Lion, once known as the Jolly Sailor. Whilst local fishermen still fish for herring, the income these days is slender. A former landlord was Robert Yeo on whom Charles Kingsley, the writer who grew up in the village, based one of the main characters in his famous novel '*Westward Ho!*' And, in a way, that seems to sum up the charm of this lovely place, there is such a subtle blend of fact and fiction here that it's hard to differentiate between them.

Drewsteignton — Devon

Drewsteignton, perched high on a ridge above the Teign gorge, has Dartmoor as a misty moorland backdrop. Despite its proximity to the A30, there is a feeling of remoteness about this Devon village, with its cob walls and thatch roofs, which is hard to define; perhaps it is because many of the houses face defensively into the square, as if sheltering from an increasingly intruding world. One group always welcome is the Mid-Devon Hunt that has been meeting here regularly since the early 1600s. It features in the *Guinness Book of Records* as if rivalling Drewsteignton's entry in the Domesday Book.

It was the Normans who gave it its name Drogo, after the Lord of the Manor. Drewe

is the name still found today on the village pub, but the Drewe Arms is no ordinary pub: inside there's not a bar as such, just a room in which to drink. It is rather like going into someone's home. I suppose in a way that is exactly what happens when you pay a visit to The Drewe Arms. There you come across Aunt Mabel, Britain's oldest landlady. It is seventy plus years ago that she pulled her first pint at the Drewe Arms.

Aunt Mabel – photograph by Chris Chapman

Prices of beer have certainly changed over the years. Now well into her nineties, Aunt Mabel remembers the days when beer was 2½d a pint and cigarettes 1½d a packet – prices difficult, if not impossible, to relate to today.

Drewsteignton's Holy Trinity Church is full of treasures; the old clock is particularly fascinating. It has been here a long time and seen better days, but wouldn't you if you had been working continuously for five hundred years, because that's how old it is. All its life it has been anonymous because it has no face and no hands. However it did strike the tenor bell on the hour, so everyone knew the time.

Talking of bells and bell ringers, it seems that they were a load of rascals, according to the ancient articles on display. One states that, 'Whoever in this place shall swear, sixpence he shall pay there fore,' and another, 'He that brings there in his hat, threepence he shall pay for that.'

There are two blocks of seats given in memory of Julius Drewe who built Castle Drogo, now a National Trust property, about a mile away from the village. The castle was designed by renowned architect Sir Edwin Lutyens and completed in 1930. To Julius Drewe, who made a fortune by importing tea for his chain of 'Home and Colonial' shops, goes the honour of building the last English castle, a magnificent achievement happily brought about by our humble need for a cup of tea!

East Coker — Somerset

East Coker, some three miles from Yeovil, is one of many Somerset villages beautifully enhanced by local golden-coloured Ham stone and thatched roofs. Where better to find an ancient craft being practised? Once an almost dying art, the thatcher's trade is today attracting young craftsmen. One young local thatcher started when he first left school at sixteen, and after a 4½ year's apprenticeship still enjoys his craft. He does not actually make the little animals that go on the ridge but buys them, although many thatchers still do make their own.

It must be something of a surprise to discover that, amidst all the Ham stone, the village hostelry is colour-washed with a slate roof. The Helyer Arms takes its name from the Helyer family, who for centuries lived at Coker Court – an early fifteenth century house that has been continuously enlarged and extended over the years. The Tudor part with its great pointed windows is in complete contrast to the Georgian wing with its large rectangular windows and stylized formality. Together with the parish church, the Court forms part of an attractive architectural group that would be hard to improve upon. This delightful group is enhanced by the Helyer Almshouses put up in 1640 as accommodation for the poor and needy of the parish. With their gable dormers and mullion windows they look as fresh as the day that they were first built.

Although the village forms part of south east Somerset's rich agricultural background, I wondered whether it had lost its farming identity in recent years? A local farmer told me that many years ago, all the field work was done with horses and most of the village folk were involved in agriculture.

Farming, however, was the last thing in the mind of local boy William Dampier, whose home was Hymerford House, a fine thatched Tudor Hall. His horizons extended far beyond the village boundary; the world was his oyster. By the time he died in 1715 he had circumnavigated the globe three times, rescued Robinson Crusoe from his desert island and discovered Australia.

The memorial that tells his story can be found in the parish church. It is in pristine condition as if it had been placed there yesterday.

Another memorial is to world-famous poet, T. S. Eliot. He was interred here in 1965 for he had strong connections with the village. His family had emigrated to America 300 years ago; he traced them back to the village and here wrote his famous poem about East Coker, called '*East Coker*'. What I love so much is that the first and last poignant lines of that poem are quoted on the memorial: 'In my beginning is my end and in my end is my beginning.'

Perhaps the best way to see East Coker is to get a rooftop view! Here we have thatchers Pete Hindle and Daniel Munroe at work on Tellis Farm Cottage. Oliver decided to keep his four feet firmly planted on the ground!

ℱeock — Cornwall

Feock in Cornwall takes its name from St Feock who, so legend would have us believe, sailed into Carrick Roads on a boulder; some say it was a mill stone. Not so improbable when you consider that early boats used discarded mill wheels as a base for their main mast. For once, a legend becomes a plausible fact.

There is some doubt as to the gender of St Feock. A local historian told me that records vary, some declaring the saint to be a woman whilst others state the reverse.

There is nothing in doubt about the village itself. Like so many of Cornwall's coastal settlements, it splits into two parts: church town situated on the hill; the waterside area, bordering the low beach and the creek, once a busy little port. Sadly, viral disease has taken its toll of Cornwall's oysters and oystering between October and 1 March has declined over the years. Oyster smacks no longer pack the creek as they used to.

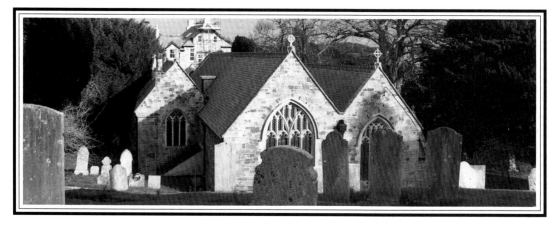

Church town groups attractively around the church, and many of the delightful cottages, with their colour-washed walls and thatched roofs, have a feel of Devon rather than Cornwall about them. Sadly, the village school, a substantial granite building, was closed in 1983, 136 years after it was founded. Life was tougher for the children in those days. They used to have to bring their pasties to school and heat them on the stove, then they would go down to the beach to help their fisherman fathers bringing in the fish. Alternatively they were obliged to return home during the lunch hour to work on their parents' farms.

The free-standing bell tower is all that is left of the thirteenth century church, and it perches high and proud on the edge of the churchyard. It served a secondary purpose, for in early days it doubled as a lighthouse, guiding ships up through the estuary. Sunday worshippers are still called to services when the bell is rung. It must be lovely listening

to that bell on a Sunday, what a pity we don't hear more bells being rung, and more often!

The Victorians were terrors, renovating churches by pulling out much of the ancient medieval woodwork, which to my mind was a wicked sin. At St Feock's they went even further, starting off with good intentions during the 1840s they extended the church a little at a time and increased the seating. However, when vicar Philpotts took over the parish, he decided that he didn't like any of it, not even the actual building, and pulled it down. So the church we see now is a Victorian church, built in 1870.

Not only is St Feock an attractive place, but it also has its rarities. They don't come much rarer than the village stocks, which contain not the usual six holes but seven! Not because they had three-legged men at Feock, but because of the great connection with the sea: the seventh hole was for sailors with wooden legs!

Gittisham — Devon

Gittisham is one of Devon's villages that is protected by stringent planning controls, and with every good reason, for with its cob walls and thatched houses it is one of the most attractive in the county. The 'Git', as the little stream is known, is kept well in its place between high walls as it threads its way down the valley to the river Otter. There is no knowledge as to who or what the 'Git' was.

The village and surrounding estate has for generations been the home of the Marker family. Richard Marker, who has returned from Canada to run it, has been carrying out remarkable developments to some of the former farm buildings. Old farm buildings have been tastefully converted into residential areas and workshops.

Just opposite the farm redevelopment is St Michael's parish church, full of memorials to Richard's ancestors. There is a wonderful atmosphere in this eighteenth century church; the little box pews with their own front doors are a sort of home from home. And you needed a few home comforts, because in those days the sermons went on for ages, hours in fact, and must have been terribly boring if not sleep inducing for everyone.

As well as the pews there is a superb monument to see: it is a tomb with a black marble surround and two enormous moulded urns. As status symbols go, it takes some beating; it is the burial place of Sir Thomas Putt and his wife. It was Sir Thomas who perfected

the famous Devon apple that was named after him, the 'Tom Putt'.

His home had been Coombe House. Still owned by the Marker estate it is now a hotel run by the Boswell family. John Boswell, a descendant of the famous eighteenth century writer and biographer James Boswell, loves this delightful Elizabethan Manor House. It dates back on this site to Norman times. The actual house we see today is Elizabethan: Cromwell's men burnt part of it, for it was a Royalist stronghold in those days. The damage was repaired in keeping with the Elizabethan style. With its wonderful collections of paintings and beautiful carvings, particularly in the hall and public rooms, it has more the appearance and feeling of a friendly country house and does not look in the least like a hotel. A charming place in which guests feel more like members of a house-party than hotel guests.

Tom Putt's original apple tree is somewhere in the grounds, well worth searching for in the autumn, if only for a modest reward in the shape of a delicious Tom Putt apple!

Hinton St George — Somerset

Most villages grow up around the Manor House, and as the Lords of the Manor prospered, so the village developed and shared their prosperity. Hinton St George in Somerset is just such a place, an estate village. The Poulletts were Lords of the Manor from the fifteenth to the present century, when the estate was sold. Now split up into

several residential units, it was originally purchased from the Poulletts by John Berkley and his wife Anne. I wondered why John had bought a house almost the size of a royal palace. Apparently it was because he was trying to get planning permission to use it as a wild life park. However, instead of having lions he hoped to house dolphins inside the building. He did not get planning permission, but ironically today, twenty years later, he would not only have received permission but also have obtained a government grant as well.

The enormous size of the place is well illustrated by a story Anne loves to tell. During the Civil War, a regiment of royalist troopers hid in the huge cellars, together with their horses, and was not discovered by searching roundheads!

Involvement in the nation's history is never far removed from the village's doorstep. The parish church is full of memorials to illustrious members of the Poullett family. Sir Ammbeous II, for example, played an important role in this country's history as the gaoler of Mary Queen of Scots, refusing to have her murdered in accordance with Elizabeth I's

wishes. We all know Mary's fate when she ceased to be his responsibility.

There is an amazing family memorial, constructed almost entirely of plaster, by continental craftsmen dating from the seventeenth century. For me however, the most fascinating thing of all is the model of the church. What is so unusual is that it is made entirely from natural materials: stone, wood, all the things you expect to find in a church including a lead roof. Made in 1844 it is built with a very soft stone called soap stone. The stone is easy to work which explains the beautifully carved parapet and gargoyles on top of the tower. The whole thing is capped by the golden weather cock.

The village is full of delightful period Ham stone houses. Looking down on it from the church tower, it is as if the barrier of time disappears: we could be seeing sixteenth century Hinton. All life's pettiness fades as we admire man's contribution to the landscape successfully achieved centuries ago without a town planner in sight!

Ilchester — Somerset

Many villages develop into towns: the reverse rarely happens. One such place however, which has seen this reversal of roles, is Ilchester in Somerset. During Roman times, it was one of the most important towns in Britain lying then as it still does on the Fosse Way, the Roman equivalent of a modern motorway.

In its time it has been a Royal Mint, a county town, home of the notorious county gaol and a Borough returning two Members of Parliament.

Today, it has the status of a large village. But why did an important Roman town develop here? Simply because it was the natural convergence of two roads and also a river crossing. The Romans built two forts here amongst good farm land, which supported the forts and villagers and in turn the forts provided protection for the farmers.

Sadly, there remains little of Roman Ilchester for us to see, just the basic street pattern. There are however strong signs of medieval Ilchester. The town trustees have renovated the ancient town hall, and in it is housed the town mace, which dates from 1250. It is the oldest mace in England, possibly the oldest mace in Europe. Its head depicts the three biblical kings and an angel covered in gold. It is thought to have been a royal gift to Ilchester.

From medieval times until its closure in 1843, Ilchester gaol was notorious. Prisoners were abused and hangings took place daily; it was no wonder inmates were always attempting to escape from this dreadful place. One man succeeded in spectacular fashion. His two sisters came to visit him in his cell; there and then they hatched the plot that involved him changing clothes with one of the sisters. He successfully escaped disguised as a lady!

All that remains of the grim group of buildings, which made up the prison, are the laundry and bakehouse, now converted into attractive cottages. I'm sure a restless spirit or two haunt those buildings! If ever a ghost was going to walk anywhere it has to be around here!

There were six churches here at one time, and just as many pubs. Several of the latter remain, but only St Mary's church with its octagonal tower is left. Inside is an unusual piece of furniture, a beautiful chest that belonged to the trustees of the almshouse charity. It has five locks, and each trustee had a key, therefore it could only be opened when all five trustees were present.

Aircraft are the basis of Ilchester's present economy, for less than a mile away is RNAS Yeovilton with its famous Fleet Air Arm Museum. Ilchester has its share of married quarters, so the military have returned once more some 1,600 years after the last Roman garrison left.

Jacobstow — Cornwall

The church tower of Jacobstow in Cornwall stands at the centre of a long thin parish. Over the years the church has, like a mother hen, gathered some attractive dwellings around it. The name Jacobstow means 'James' town', and sure enough the parish church, with its wondrous tower soaring amidst the trees and memorial stones, which flank the churchyard, is dedicated to St James.

I just love these village churchyards with their grave stones: pocket handkerchief-size biographies of people who once lived in the village years ago. Originally graves were not as we see them today, they were just simple humps in the ground marked with wooden crosses. But the wood rotted and families were unable to identify their ancestors' graves, so they chose instead stone crosses with their names carved on them. Such memorials were usually made by the village stonemason who, finding it difficult to work outside during the winter months, carved a selection of stones and crosses. He then added the name of the deceased when the occasion arose. The most unusual, as well as the most

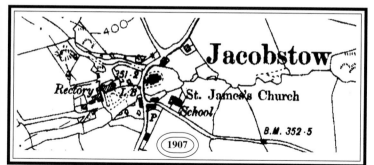

attractive stone, is based on 'Three Little Pigs Went to Market'.

The resonant tones of the organ filled the church on the day of my visit. The organist, Mollie Parsons, who is also the parish clerk and church warden, was practising for the Sunday service: a lovely welcoming sound. The church boasts some unusual possessions, including an altar stone brought in from the churchyard in 1972. It had been taken from the church many years before at the time of the Reformation and deposited outside. It has several fine features, including the original cross carved on the top. Mollie Parsons was married to the local blacksmith, and she still lives in the cottage beside the old forge.

Strangely, for such a small village, there is a large modern school here: a school that serves four surrounding villages. All four original schools were closed down and a brand new school built. The children find plenty to do with their spare time: they are able to go on woodland walks and see badger cubs and enjoy the countryside. The majority told me that they would like to stay in their village when they grow up, a fine testimony to village life. With new homes being built which blend in with the lovely old cottages, it certainly does look as if all will be well for Jacobstow in the future.

King's Nympton — North Devon

King's Nympton, a hilltop village in North Devon, takes its name from the Celtic word 'nematon' meaning sacred grove, once the King's grove. This is something I discovered, not in the history books, but by studying the pub sign of the suitably named 'Grove Inn', a hostelry unique in so far as it was once also the village post office. A village full of attractive houses and unspoilt cottages, many of them have delightful names. I was particularly taken by the Victorian house that used to be the village Police Station!

Lying as it does well off any main road, virtually untouched by time, King's Nympton seems to embody all that is perfect in the English village. It has the appearance of a chocolate-box cover, without the attendant cloying sweetness. Making my way around the village, I kept catching tantalizing glimpses of the distinctive copper spire of the parish church.

In the churchyard I joined Ken Avery who had lived in the village all his life. He can

trace his family back in the same village to about 1770, a fact that becomes obvious as you note the family names on several of the headstones among the myriad that fill the churchyard. Many of Ken's ancestors have worshipped at the parish church over the centuries.

The inside there is rather special. There are tiered seats, which is unusual because of the way they rise up at the back of the church. This was because the church orchestra used to sit there in the days before they had an organ, so the orchestra sat on the raised seats with the choir in front of them. This elevated position gives one a chance to see the rest of the church, dominated by a superb rood screen. By far the most unusual thing I have ever seen, rare in any church, is a separate ceiling to the rood, called a cellular ceiling. It is quite beautiful. Beyond that again is the chancel's painted ceiling, unique in so far as it was a 'do it yourself' job by the local vicar back in 1755.

King's Nympton is a lovely place, well worth a visit on a sunny day, or any other day for that matter.

Lustleigh — Devon

Some villages are as indifferent to time passing as the stone from which they are built, and Lustleigh on the very edge of Dartmoor is such a place. Renowned for its ancient May Day ceremony and picturesque cottages, its name is derived from the Saxon, and means 'south of the wood'.

The village developed around the sloping village green. In the centre is a fine cross, a memorial to Henry Tudor: not Henry VIII but a local vicar of the same name and much more sober of habit. Primrose Cottage is a famous award winning tea room. Being at the centre of a conservation area I would have thought the village had little chance of being changed. But former dairyman and village special constable Eddie Ellis worries that too many houses are becoming second homes or holiday lets, ousting many of the 'old characters' of the village.

Dominating the centre of the village is the fifteenth century granite church, and in the

churchyard is Lustleigh's one and only street lamp. And what a beauty, it is Victorian and made of cast iron.

The church porch is quite rare because it is long and deep. The reason for this is that it originally acted as the parish hall. Villagers held meetings here, courts were held, and schoolchildren were even taught the 'three Rs'. The most intriguing features are the two unusual holes in the wall. No one seems to know what their purpose was, but I suspect that they were holes through which lepers took the Holy Sacrament. What they must have done was to pull back the tiny sliding door, look inside, and then take the sacrament.

The 1937 May Queen celebrations

Village life always seems to revolve around both the church and the pub. The Cleave Hotel, once a farmhouse, is the local hostelry and a fine building.

Lustleigh is one of those villages that was fortunate to survive the great Plague that swept the country during the fourteenth century, mainly because it was surrounded by a river and the rodents could not get across. To celebrate their good fortune, the villagers decided that every year on May Day they would have a 'festival' and elect a Queen. The Queen's throne is in the orchard, and carved on that throne are the names of all the May Queens since 1954.

Apparently things do not always run smoothly on May Day. One former queen recounted to me how at her ceremony a goat broke loose and started eating all the flowers adorning her throne; before he could be stopped, he started on the canopy of flowers! The children were singing well but they could not be heard because the crowd were laughing so much!

Even if you can't make the ceremony, there is so much else to see at Lustleigh, including delightful buildings like the old school. Do go along and have a look for yourself.

The 1954 May Queen, seen here, is Gillian Williams, daughter of the 1937 May Queen shown on the previous page!

Montacute — Somerset

For a moment or two you wonder why the buildings of Montacute in Somerset are so much in harmony with one another, then it comes to you: they are all built of the rich golden stone quarried from nearby Ham Hill. The village takes its name from the very steep hill 'Mons Acutis' which, overgrown with trees, seems to loom almost menacingly over the village. Once the site of a Norman castle, today it is capped by a glorious folly tower.

At the foot of the hill is a magnificent gate house, all that is left of the thirteenth century Cluniac Priory, now a farm and the home of Major and Mrs Jenkins. The huge arch of the actual gateway opening has been tastefully restored and is fully glazed, blending old and new and enabling the family to enjoy views of the gardens. Renovated in this highly original way, the character of the archway has been preserved without harming the stone work in any way.

The village developed around the 'borough', a perfect square and one of the earliest of its type in Europe. Montacute has in its time been quite an innovator in one way or another. Have you ever wondered what the first rural council houses looked like, or where they were built? Well, they were put up by the Yeovil Rural District Council in Montacute at Townsend in 1912. Now most of them have been sold to tenants. Solidly built of local Ham stone, they are appreciated by owners and passers-by alike.

Today the church, beautifully set within its churchyard, is peaceful. But it was not always so. One of the favourite sports and pastimes of the late seventeenth and early eighteenth centuries was the playing of 'fives' up against blank walls. Frequently the church tower walls were used, and that is exactly what happened at Montacute. Unfortunately the games got out of hand and players went wild. They cracked tiles, broke windows and damaged the stonework. Eventually the church authorities banned them and the game was taken over by the pubs, who built their own special walls. What is so interesting is that, in order to make a smooth playing surface, the rascals chipped off the decorative string course!

Inside are the tombs of the Phelips family, builders of the village's great pride and joy, Montacute House, surely the finest Elizabethan Mansion in the country. Started towards the end of the sixteenth century, it too is built of golden Ham stone, as are the Gazebos – ornate summer houses set in delightful gardens. Beautifully maintained by the National Trust, it is open to visitors and, like the village itself, is well worth a visit.

𝕹ewton and 𝕹oss — 𝕯evon

Newton Ferrers and Noss Mayo, shortened to Newton and Noss, sound like a famous comedy team such as Laurel and Hardy or Morecombe and Wise, and in a way that is what they are – inseparable. They peer across a side creek of the river Yealm in South Devon at each other in open admiration. And with good reason, for as waterside villages go they are absolutely charming. The steep hillsides sloping down to the water are packed with trees interspersed with modern dwellings, whilst the creek is lined with old fishermen's cottages. Fish as well as tin were once exported to France from here in exchange for wine, salt and pottery, bringing enormous prosperity to this part of South Devon. Today it is a haven for yachtsmen, and the creek is graced with boats of every shape, size and and colour.

The steep, narrow streets of Newton lead directly to the waterside, where even narrower streets run parallel to the creek. What is so fascinating, as well as unusual, is the way in which the front gardens are separated from the houses by the road: independent plots of land with a delightful river view. Incidentally, the pub's 'Gents' follows the same pattern. It too is across the road; so is the reading room, a relic of Victorian times when papers as well as books were expensive. So folk with little cash to spare took advantage of the 'freebies' available, that is of course if they were able to read!

Noss church is Victorian, designed by Piers St Aubyn, the architect ancestor of the family who owned St Michael's Mount in Cornwall. Newton church is much older,

having been built in 1300 on even earlier foundations. The church includes some unusual features. It may look like any other church inside but there is a subtle difference. The nave is perfectly straight as far as the chancel arch but it then cants off to the right. Legend has it that Christ's head fell to the right on the cross and that is why it is built in this manner. It becomes very apparent as you look up through the nave. Personally I think there is more to it than that – I reckon the builder got his measurements wrong!

There is a hagioscope, which is a rather 'posh' name for a squint, providing a glimpse of the altar for people who sat in the side aisles. Sedilia is an equally 'posh' name for the three seats in the chancel. They are upmarket seats, because you would not normally expect to find them in a parish church; usually they are to be found in Cathedrals or Abbeys. The normal arrangement was that the priest sat in the first one and gave the sermon, the deacon sat in the second one and he read the epistle, whilst the sub-deacon sat in the third one; his job was to read the lesson.

Across the road from the church I found seats of a different sort. They were much more popular at the time of my visit; they were in a restaurant selling Devonshire's greatest gift to the culinary arts: the Devon Cream Tea! Having lived all my life in the South West, I still haven't found the answer to the greatest mystery of all: which do you put on the scone first – the jam or the cream?

Oare — Somerset

I have always felt that when you'd seen one moor you'd seen them all. Exmoor however is quite different, probably because it broods over a valley from which menace once emanated, for we are in Doone country. As you look around it seems only right that R. D. Blackmore's famous story *'Lorna Doone'*, considered the greatest selling novel of all time, should be set here in the South West. Is the book based on the truth or not? After all there were Doones: Lorna married John Ridd, and Carver Doone did shoot someone by that name. The valley, Badgeworthy Water, the farm and the church do exist, as does Oare.

The hamlet is far from being a fictional place, and visitors from all over the world arrive with one question in their minds: is it fact or fiction? There is supposed to be a legend in which robbers used to inhabit the remote parts, but as is often the case it is always very difficult to distinguish fact from fiction. Today, Lorna Doone farm still stands beside the ancient pack horse bridge and ford at Malmsmead. Now a souvenir shop, it sells, amongst other goodies, copies of 'The Book'. It is also a fine garden centre, packed with a variety of heathers as well as a large selection of flowering plants and shrubs.

Beside the church is Oare Manor, a grand building that features in the novel. Apparently Blackmore first heard the story of the Doones from his grandfather who was Rector back in the eighteenth century. What is interesting is that the Doones and the Ridds are recorded in church records. Although some of those records have disappeared, there is a more tangible record for some of the Ridds are buried in the church yard.

The church, dating from the fifteenth century, is a very simple structure. Inside, it has a wagon roof, Georgian box pews and a simple screen. The most famous incident in the

book took place at the chancel steps. John Ridd was about to marry his beloved Lorna when a shot rang out and she collapsed at his feet. That shot was fired by a jealous Carver Doone from a window in the church and, just in case you've never read the story, I am not going to tell you the outcome. Rumour has it however that Blackmore based it on another incident at Chagford in Devon, where Mary Whiddon suffered a similar experience.

Do visit Oare and buy a copy of the book for yourself. I should not like to deprive R. D. Blackmore of his royalties! I know he died in 1900, but his relations still benefit. To be honest, people visit Oare mainly to find out whether the book is fact or fiction. Why else should the world and his wife make a journey to this little Somerset village?

Whilst it is difficult to authenticate the Lorna Doone story, I have a theory that the answer lies in the name of the place: it's not Oare but 'Oh arr' the Somerset dialect way of saying, 'Yes'.

Portloe — Cornwall

It seems as though time has stood still at Portloe. Hemmed in by tremendous dark cliffs, it has kept to itself over the centuries, preserving it as the least spoiled and certainly the most impressive fishing village in Cornwall. Portloe grew up around the tiny creek, with just a few cottages at the water's edge above fish cellars, a couple of which are still here: man-made caves aping nature's efforts in the surrounding cliffs.

Today the nucleus of the village is a conservation area, and rightly so too. Only one new house appears to have been built in the immediate harbour area since the turn of the century.

In its heyday, which would have been about the late 1800s, the village had its own band, choir, cricket and football teams, all supported by a brisk trade in crab and lobster, brought in by some sixty or more fishing boats. There are several retired fishermen in Portloe who

have fished here all their lives. Before the Second World War there were some thirty working boats. Indeed, even after the War there were still the same number, but since then they have steadily dwindled until today there are just six boats.

Times do change – even some of buildings take on a new life. The Lugger Hotel, once a smugglers' inn, is now very much connected with the holiday industry, and the rest of the village has followed suit. More geared up to holidays rather than fishing, the whole village appears to depend on the holiday trade: the Lugger and the Ship Inn both rely on tourists, and almost fifty per cent of the houses in the village are self catering or holiday homes.

Signs of past importance and prosperity are everywhere. Most of the former coastguard cottages are now holiday homes, whilst the original boathouse for the customs cutter is now a beautifully converted house, complete with the original launching ramp.

The parish church is not all it seems, it too has strong maritime connections: for six years it was the lifeboat house. The first time the lifeboat was launched, it crashed into a shop, providing more of an emergency on shore than the one they were attending to out at sea! It is not surprising that this delightful place, still a fishing community though much smaller than it was, is so attractive to holidaymakers and artists alike. May it continue unspoilt forever.

Queen Camel — Somerset

Queen Camel in Somerset is a delightful village with a lovely name, a name that it takes from 'A hill over looking the village. The high narrow hill in a manor owned by the Queen,' or Queen Camel for short. The long wide main street is packed with delightful houses, many covered with thatched roofs. The grey stone is enlivened by dressings around the doors and windows of golden Ham stone from nearby Ham Hill. The street picture is enlivened even more by a superb example of topiary, a huge bird, hedge cutting par excellence.

I always think houses are like human beings: basically the same, but individually quite different. You won't find a more perfect illustration of that opinion than the houses lining the streets of Queen Camel. The ones with dormer windows seem to be raising their eyebrows as if to question your presence, whereas others with large windows seem to be welcoming you with a smile.

The streets are not all wide at Queen Camel. The superb cobbled way leading to the church has been restored by this enterprising village, with individuals as well as groups making their contributions. One contributor was Sir Denis Thatcher, husband of the former prime minister. One of his ancestors Peter Thatcher was vicar in the lovely parish church back in the seventeenth century.

QUEEN CAMEL. S.C.

The church is full of beautiful things that have been added over the centuries. The lights, though modern, fit in well, whilst the rood screen dates from the 1500s. The carved beams holding up the roof are a rarity in a parish church and are a great treasure. The font is absolutely marvellous. Nearly six hundred years old, it is unusual because it has a column on each corner with little figures of angels on each one. But once again, Oliver Cromwell's louts came along and knocked the heads off because they did not approve of what they called 'idols' in a church. Another interesting thing is that font water was holy water, and in the Middle Ages people would steal the water, witches in particular using it for black magic purposes. This did not go down at all well with the clergy, so the then Archbishop of Canterbury said that all fonts should have lockable lids. This one has a beautiful but quite modern lid dated 1959, proving that craftsmanship is not dead.

It is certainly not dead in this village because Keith Robinson has his workshop in the main street, and he is a furniture maker with an international reputation. He reckons that the village craftsman has to work much harder today than those of years ago, mainly because he cannot obtain the quality materials, although he feels that modern craftsmen are often superior to their predecessors. With craftsmen of Keith's calibre about, the skills rooted in the traditional English craft will never die. Nor for that matter will the English village, of which Queen Camel is such a perfect example. For here, whilst they are building new houses, they are also preserving the identity by skilfully converting barns into superb 'traditional' dwellings.

Rampisham — Dorset

Rampisham has one of the loveliest pack horse bridges in Dorset. Fully arched, it is a narrow bridge just wide enough to take one pony, and of course it has low parapets in order to clear the load swung on either side of the pack horses. It leads to one of the most delightful villages in Dorset, Rampisham. The village originally took its name from Rame or Rane, a Saxon landowner. By the eighteenth century the population had increased to about 430, it has dwindled today to about 150.

Whilst cottages have been demolished over the years, several lovely ones still remain. Amongst them is the post office, a delightful thatched cottage, which still has the ancient pump outside with the date 1793 emblazoned on a lead panel.

Pugin Hall, the former rectory, is a rare architectural gem. It was designed as a rectory by the splendidly named Augustus Welby Northmore Pugin, the famous Victorian architect who, amongst other great works, was responsible for the interior design of the Houses of Parliament. It is now a family home, and the present owners have copies of the original working drawings for the house. The rectory, including the architect's fees, cost £1,926.8s.0d. when it was built in 1846.

The Manor House, much older, was at one time a monastery, which has been added to over the years, with the bulk of the new work taking place back in 1608. It stands below the parish church, which was restored by Pugin at the same time as he was working on the rectory. In the church yard, the base is all that remains of a preaching cross. The large shaft, topped by a stone cross, has long since gone. Visiting preachers would give sermons, marry couples and even commit Christians to burial from such crosses, for very often there was just a cross – the actual church was put up later. What is unique about this particular churchyard is the presence of a stone table, which was known as a dole table. From it the poor of the parish received a free supply of bread.

St Just in Roseland — Cornwall

Cornwall, a county of great beauty, surpasses even itself in St Just in Roseland. Surprisingly the name has nothing to do with roses. It comes from the old Cornish word Ruse meaning promontory, St Just being one of the early Cornish hermits who probably lived here.

Legend has it that the young Jesus Christ landed here with his uncle Joseph of Arimathea, and quite frankly the atmosphere of this sacred place is such that it certainly makes their presence here quite believable. (Christ in the South West is covered in detail in my book More…Cobblestones, Cottages and Castles.)

The little creek just off Carrick Roads has certainly played its part in the nation's history. During the 1800s it was a quarantine port for Falmouth just across the estuary. Ships rested here after Trafalgar, and at the turn of this century it was very nearly the site of a new naval base. Mercifully Devonport was chosen instead.

The village stands high on a hill overlooking the creek, and the charming colour-rendered cottages glow in the sunlight.

The churchyard looks more like a huge, beautiful, quite perfect Cornish garden, and is considered to be the finest churchyard in the world. There is hardly a level meter in it as

it tumbles down towards church and creek, full of sub-tropical plants, trees and shrubs, which thrive in the gentle climate of this part of Cornwall. They owe their presence to John Tresidder; he provided them on his return from Australia in 1897.

The lower lych gate, or what was called the corpse gate (the word lych meant corpse) is where the coffin was brought by boat and laid in the middle sheltered by the porch; the actual committal service started here. However the one at St Just is rather different: there is a series of stones forming a grid across it and this is what is known as a Cornish stile, specifically to keep animals out of the churchyard.

One of the earliest churches in Britain, St Just's dates from Celtic times and is simply beautiful inside. There are some intriguing features. There is a little tiny sink that was used to wash the vessels after the communion service and is called a piscina. Perhaps even more interesting is that you can still see just above the piscina the joint between the older section and the later built church.

The village provides stewards who give their time free to stay in the church ready to welcome any one who may have a problem. They are always there, not so much to talk but simply to listen and offer help. Anyone seeking peace will certainly find it here in this lovely place.

Thorverton — Devon

The village name Thorverton literally means 'A ford marked by a thorn bush.' Well, the ford is still here, but the thorn bush has long since gone; the charming little bridge is of much more recent date. Not so the village however, for it goes back well over a thousand years. Owned for several centuries by successive monarchs, it was eventually given by Edward I to the Dean and Chapter of Exeter Cathedral. They inherited the delightful church of St Thomas à Becket, which was built as an act of penance by William de Tracy, one of the Knights who assassinated Becket at Canterbury Cathedral.

The church has a carillon that plays hymns regularly at midday; a lovely sound that regularly fills the village with its delicate chimes. There is an unusual little room over the porch called a 'parvis'. It is a place where the priest lived centuries ago. This single room then served as a bedroom, kitchen and dining room that contained little more than a table, a bed, a lamp and his books. A forerunner of the vicarage.

The bedroom over the porch of the village butcher's shop is more generous in size. The

fine building dated 1763 has been in the same family for generations. However one wonders how long the traditional village shop and the service they provide will last?

One service, however, not likely to fade away is the village pub. Thorverton is well blessed indeed for it has three of them. The eighteenth century 'Dolphin' stands on what was once a busy cross-roads. Before then the Exeter road was realigned to the East. That move allowed the village to survive and remain unspoilt.

Many houses remain unchanged and still have their thatched roofs and rendered cob walls. In the centre of the village close to the church is a perfect example of cob walling: red local mud held together with straw and the occasional odd stone or two popped in. It has stood like this for centuries, almost as good as stone. It was the cob wall that brought about the thatched roof; cob was not strong enough to hold up stone or tiled roofs so thatch, being that much lighter, was used.

One of the oldest buildings is a fourteenth century farmhouse, now the post office. Inside is an ancient fireplace. It dates from 1600 when the roof of the house was raised and the fireplace installed. The remains of the bread oven are still here, and an unusual pointed shaped kettle, which was filled with beer and poked into the embers of the fire to warm it, hence warm beer for a cold day!

This is essentially a quiet village, and so lovely that I personally feel that it deserves more visitors.

Ugborough — South Devon

Ugborough is a lovely place, with what sounds like an unattractive name. But all is well, for it means 'Uggers Hill', the name of the original Lord of the Manor. Approaching the village, you pass Ware Farm, a charming group of buildings that dates back many centuries. The village developed around a large square, with the church standing on slightly high ground. This is because it was built on a prehistoric earth work, so there has been a settlement of sorts here for thousands of years. The second biggest parish in Devon, it is full of delightful houses and cottages. The tiny building in the square is a bricked-in conduit, which used to provide fresh water for the village. The delightful 'Donkey Lane' acquired its name from a former vicar who came this way to church on his donkey. However, donkeys no longer reign supreme in Donkey Lane: other residents today include a friendly parrot as well as several cats and dogs.

The church is larger than most parish churches, apparently it was once considered to be a local 'cathedral'. Inside are some intriguing features that have stood the passage of time. I am always fascinated by the way in which sayings of the old days have been adopted into the English language. Most of them seem to have originated in churches. For example, in medieval times the whole of the floor space of the church was clear: there were no seats or any form of seating. Rushes were strewn about and people stood for the service, except the very old and very young. What they did for them was to provide a stone seat running around the perimeter of the wall. That is where we get the well known saying 'Weakest to the Wall'.

On the lower panels of the rood screen are some of the oldest paintings in the South West; the illustrations are mainly of angels. An unusual one is of the man who beheaded John the Baptist, and it has clearly been disfigured. In Cromwellian times they scratched out the faces, because it was felt to be heretical to have graven images in church.

The village had two pubs, the 'Ship' and the 'Anchor'. These names are said to have been derived from the fact that Ugborough was the farthest place sailors could reach from their ships anchored at Devonport and get back in one night. Another similar theory was

that they were just out of reach of the press-gangs. It is an interesting thought that press-gangs can still be formed today to press men into the Navy if there is a shortage of sailors, for that law has never been repealed.

Older residents of Ugborough are particularly proud of their village, as it is one of best kept villages in Devon.

Veryan — Cornwall

Villages sometimes grew up around the manor house, often at the whim of the Lord of the Manor, and in a way that is what happened at Veryan. The village splits into two parts either side of the big house, simply because the Tryst family did not want village dwellings too close to their estate. At either end of the village are pairs of round houses, looking like the gateway to a medieval town. And in a way they served a similar purpose, for they served as lodges to the estate. They were built by parson Jeremiah Tryst as homes for his five daughters for, apart from those at the entrances to Veryan, there is a fifth house in the centre of the village. They cost just £50 each to build in 1811. I spoke to one village resident who was actually born in one of them in 1892!

The village is named after St Buryan, and as the letters B and V are interchangeable in the Cornish language, this is probably why it is called Veryan today. The more conventional houses are traditionally Cornish, and they huddle together around the green at the Northern end of the village. The delightful garden, which adjoins the churchyard, was the gift of one man in memory of his wife.

In the churchyard of St Symphorian parish church I made a fascinating discovery: the Tryst family vault. It has a marvellous stately entrance, more worthy of Highgate or Kensel Green Cemeteries in London than a small parish church, and the whole thing is constructed of Cornish granite. Its most fascinating feature is the panel containing names of all the Tryst family, which includes four of the five daughters for whom the round

houses were built. The longest grave ever recorded in any churchyard is here at Veryan. Although only one metre (3 feet) wide it is forty metres (130 feet) long, for buried head to toe are 19 crew members of the *Hera*, a German barque that sank off the coast in 1914. There appears to be no explanation why the grave was elongated in this way, for normally coffins are placed side by side in communal graves.

Inside the church, much of which was built during the fifteenth century, is an unusual memorial to other seamen who lost their lives around the treacherous coast. It is a beautiful model of a ship.

A more tangible and practical link are the Homeyard Homes, a group of modern buildings, the design of which has been based on the ancient round houses. They are mostly occupied by seamen's widows. One occupant has been in residence since they were first built, but over the years it has not always been possible to find seamen's widows. However, the houses are never left vacant as there is a points system, rather like the council house system. Other folk, not necessarily connected with the sea, can now be considered.

My visit coincided with the church fête, an essential part of village life. And on the basis that one good turn deserves another (the vicar having told me about the history of the Homeyard Homes) I was invited to open the church fête. You know, one never hears of a pub having to hold a fête to pay for a new roof, it is always a church that has to raise money for such things. Long live the tradition of the annual village fête!

𝖂𝖍𝖎𝖙𝖈𝖍𝖚𝖗𝖈𝖍 𝕮𝖆𝖓𝖔𝖓𝖎𝖈𝖔𝖗𝖚𝖒 — 𝕯𝖔𝖗𝖘𝖊𝖙

In medieval times, all roads in Dorset led to Whitchurch Canonicorum. At that time churches and cathedrals were full of shrines, which contained the bones of a patron saint, at which miracle cures took place. After the Reformation most were destroyed. Just two remain: that of Edward the Confessor in Westminster Abbey, and Saint Wita's shrine in Dorset. The village name, Whitchurch, seems to have been derived from 'white church': the tower, although golden in colour, would have been considered white in comparison to Saxon church towers, which were usually built of timber. There is a serenity here which seems to have built up over the centuries through the visits of countless pilgrims.

Saint Wita's shrine is apparently some nine hundred years old, and her body is in the top section. In 1900 a crack appeared in the tomb, and on it being opened up they found the bones of a woman. So it was confirmed that Saint Wita was a lady, but very little else could be found out about her. Pilgrims came to Whitchurch to be cured, and it is recorded that many were, from the Middle Ages onwards. What the pilgrims did was to place their injured sick limbs into one of the three holes in the tomb and pray to be cured. This still occurs today: people come to the church and place post cards in the holes, with their prayer for the sick. These cards are taken to the altar, and the people named are prayed for at a church service every week. What a nice thought that is!

It is therefore not surprising that quite large villages built up around shrines, and Whitchurch is no exception. It is full of typical Dorset cottages that hardly seem to change

over the centuries. But change does happen, and the deeds of one house in the village, for instance, show that at one time it was a public house called the 'New Inn'. In the garden across the main road is a brick built toilet with a thatched roof. Traffic must have been a hazard if you were taken short!

Whitchurch has progressed quite gently into the twentieth century. For example, a group of farm buildings has been skilfully converted into holiday accommodation.

I am quite sure that Saint Wita would be very proud of this lovely village, which owes its very presence to the fact that even today she is still exercising her role in helping the sick.

e𝔛ford — Somerset

No one, even the noble stag whose kingdom it surely is, has managed to tame Exmoor. Nor are the ponies, whose stamping ground it has been for at least a thousand years, entirely at home, for Exmoor belongs to the elements. There are few settlements of any size on Exmoor and Exford, so named as 'the ford by the river Exe,' is the largest. The dwellings group around a fine village green where, over successive centuries, fairs of every sort and size have been held. The houses too vary in shape, size and colour, and are cosmopolitan rather than being typical of the Somerset countryside.

Beside the Exe is the 'White Horse', a hostelry that, from its decor, proves that Exford's economy is based on hunting. The village has two packs of hounds, stag hounds and fox hounds. Naturally there is the usual holiday period in the summer when the visitors arrive, bolstering the economy. But if it were not for the hunts, many consider that the village would be hard put to survive. Two pubs and three shops cater for this thriving community.

Generations of huntsmen and their families are buried in the churchyard, and although the church's nave and chancel were built in Victorian times, it does have a treasure or two. The rood screen must be the most travelled in Britain. Five hundred years old, it started

life in Watchet parish Church, which is not far away. During the nineteenth century when the church was restored, the screen was removed and a new one put in. Someone had the foresight to store, rather than to destroy it. Several years later, the Watchet PCC decided to give it to the Victoria and Albert museum. Here it was restored by their craftsmen, and what a beautiful job they made of it: you can see where the damaged pieces were replaced. When Exford PCC were looking for a screen in 1929, the then Bishop of Bath and Wells remarked that he knew of one. He referred them to the Victoria and Albert, and here it stands today. They bought it for £700, which does not sound a lot nowadays, but of course then was the value of, say, three semi-detached houses, so perhaps we're talking of £150,000 by today's standards.

There is, in the church, a lovely organ with carved panels that contained marvellous pictures. If you think one or two of them are a bit racy for a church, don't worry because the instrument originally belonged to a layman and was designed for his own home by the famous Sir Ninian Comper.

The moorland surrounding Exford was an unclaimed wilderness until the government enclosed it in 1815. Three fifths of the bleak area were sold to optimistic Midlands ironmaster-cum-farmer John Knight, who thought he could tame the moor. He did his best, building fifteen new farms. Stone walls and high banks topped with trees enclosed square fields in an attempt to control the landscape. For thirty years he poured a fortune into the project, but the wilderness won. Mentally beaten and financially bankrupt, he retreated from the moor leaving it to the deer, the sheep and the Exmoor ponies, and its real master, the elements.

Yealmpton — Devon

There can not be another village in the country that has its history written and recorded in the form of a poem, the first verse of which is known to every one of us. It is the nursery rhyme 'Old Mother Hubbard' written at Yealmpton in Devon.

Sarah Martin wrote it in 1805 on a visit to her sister, who was married to Squire Bastard of nearby Kitley House. She based the character on the old lady who was the housekeeper at the time. There are a surprising 28 verses in the poem, which are little more than a list of shops and pubs. Probably the best known verse recounts how, 'The cupboard was bare,' and that 'the poor little doggy had none.' It is at this point that the rhyme also becomes a social document, for the bare cupboard refers to the great shortage of food brought about by the Napoleonic Wars.

Old Mother Hubbard eventually retired to a charming cottage still standing in the village, which, by the shape of its walls and undulating thatched roof, has to be the perfect residence for such a character.

Today the cottage is a restaurant, and customers are always surprised to learn that this delightful place was indeed the source of the nursery rhyme.

Older people in the village talk of happy and peaceful times whilst growing up in the village, and some still remember when the church tower was 'toppled' down and the ensuing fund raising to help with the rebuilding. In 1911 it was decided to pull down the tower, as it proved to be insecure and liable to fall at any minute. But how to raise the money?

The vicar, the Rev Warner, had a brainwave. He wrote a letter to all the children in the village telling of the financial problems and signing the letter 'Mother Hubbard'! The news got out, the local press getting hold

of the story, the national press followed and even the international press took it up. From all over the world donations came pouring in, the amount soon reached the £2,000 required, and the tower was rebuilt.

Many of the shops and pubs referred to in the nursery rhyme have closed. No longer are there hatters, cobblers or tailors, and even the baker has packed it in! The rhyme however tells us, 'She went to the bakers to buy some bread and when she got back the poor dog was dead.' He must have been merely faint with hunger, for 'She went to the tavern to buy white wine and red and when she came back the dog stood on his head.' And of course the rhyme does end on a happy note, the dog successfully married and in the last verse, 'The bride made a curtsy the dog made a bow, the Dame wished them joy and they both said Bow Wow!'

Zennor — Cornwall

Zennor, beginning as it does with the last letter of the alphabet, befits the letter 'Z' for it is at the end of the line – well almost anyway. Situated on the north coast of the Penwith peninsula, it is close to Land's End.

The village is bleakly situated some 350 feet above sea level, amidst heather, strewn with huge granite boulders and bereft of trees. On a wind-swept winter's morning it is a soul searching place, but on a glorious summer's day, with an emerald sea teasing the shore line, it has all the charm of the Mediterranean.

It was on such a day that renowned novelist D. H. Lawrence saw this part of Cornwall for the first time whilst staying at the Tinners' Arms. He fell in love with Zennor, and subsequently took a house here. That was during the First World War. Sadly, it was not for long. A combination of bad weather and a German wife, together with his 'alien' north country accent convinced the locals that they were German spies and they were driven away.

Neither the Cornish nor Zennor's remoteness deterred John Wesley. He apparently preached several of his 'firebrand' sermons from the great rock that overlooks the village.

Nearby is the Wayside Museum, well worth a visit: a museum with a difference. On the edge of the village is the Zennor Quoit, a pre-Christian chamber tomb that has now partially collapsed. The seven uprights are ten feet tall, and originally supported another weighing twelve tons that formed the roof.

But it is the parish church, dedicated to Saint Senara, which is the village's greatest attraction. Inside is the most

The famous 'Mermaid of Zennor'

famous bench-end in the country, depicting the mermaid of Zennor – a tale of love more emotive than any of Shakespeare's more romantic love stories, it even outdoes Mills & Boon! The story is as follows…

Sorry, I'm not going to spoil it for you! If you want to know the story it's all there in the church. Make an expedition for yourself, I promise you it will be well worth the visit.

David Young, TV presenter, architect, writer and raconteur has, for more years than he cares to remember, been travelling the South West of England with Labrador companions 'William' and latterly 'Oliver', in a series of journeys regularly shown on

Westward Diary and on *Today*, Television South West's former nightly regional news/ magazine programmes. In the programmes he looked at the region's buildings, historic follies, customs and folklore. They have taken him on horseback following the journeys of John Wesley, by Bullnose Morris to follow H. V. Morton's route across the South West, he has journeyed by stage coach, flown and sailed the coastline and even trudged it as a tramp – fascinating young and old alike with his highly personal approach to the subject.

From time to time he ventures on to the Network bringing a breath of West Country air to the rest of Britain The highly-acclaimed award-winning series *Bats in the Belfry*, an eccentric series of journeys looking at follies, off-beat buildings and strange structures, was followed by two equally successful series of *Cobblestones, Cottages and Castles*.

Curiosity has been his inspiration and entertainment his motive and now you can join him in his unique celebration of the South West in his best selling book *More Cobblestones, Cottages and Castles*. It is available in both hardback at £9.95 and softback at £6.95 from most good bookshops or direct from the publishers.

Obelisk Publications specialises in books about Devon. For further details please send an SAE to 2 Church Hill, Pinhoe, Exeter, Devon, EX4 9ER or telephone Exeter (0392) 468556.